Martin Luther KING Jr.

Martin Luther KING Jr.

by Laurie Calkhoven

Illustrated by Charlotte Ager

Editor Allison Singer
Senior Designer Joanne Clark

Project Editor Roohi Sehgal
Editor Radhika Haswani
Additional Editorial Kritika Gupta
Art Editor Kanika Kalra
Project Art Editor Yamini Panwar
Jacket Coordinator Francesca Young
Jacket Designer Joanne Clark
DTP Designers Nand Kishor Acharya,
Sachin Gupta, Vijay Kandwal
Picture Researcher Aditya Katyal
Illustrator Charlotte Ager
Pre-Producer, Pre-Production Dragana Puvacic
Producer Basia Ossowska
Managing Editors Laura Gilbert, Monica Saigal
Deputy Managing Art Editor Ivy Sengupta
Managing Art Editor Diane Peyton Jones
Delhi Team Head Malavika Talukder
Creative Director Helen Senior
Publishing Director Sarah Larter

Subject Consultant Kyair Butts
Literacy Consultant Stephanie Laird

First American Edition, 2019
Published in the United States by DK Publishing
345 Hudson Street, New York, New York 10014

Copyright © 2019 Dorling Kindersley Limited
DK, a Division of Penguin Random House LLC
19 20 21 22 23 10 9 8 7 6 5 4 3 2 1
001–308810–Jan/19

A catalog record for this book is available from the Library of Congress.
ISBN: 978-1-4654-7435-3 (Paperback)
ISBN: 978-1-4654-7542-8 (Hardcover)

DK books are available at special discounts when purchased in bulk for sales promotions,
premiums, fund-raising, or educational use. For details, contact:
DK Publishing Special Markets,
345 Hudson Street, New York, New York 10014
SpecialSales@dk.com

Printed and bound in China

A WORLD OF IDEAS:
SEE ALL THERE IS TO KNOW

www.dk.com

Dear Reader,

I was eight years old when Dr. Martin Luther King Jr. died—too young to understand fully what had happened, but old enough to know that our country had lost a great man.

In learning more about Martin's life to write this biography, I finally understood just how great he was. Martin's belief in positive change through love and non-violence made a real difference. When people around him were (understandably) reacting to racism with anger and violence, Martin held firm to his belief that only peaceful action could change the world.

I hope Martin's life will inspire you, as it has inspired me, to always "meet hate with love" and believe in your dreams to create a better world.

Laurie Calkhoven

The life of...
Martin **Luther** KiNG Jr.

Family of ministers

Early in his life, there were clues young Martin Luther King Jr. would grow up to become a leader in the fight for civil rights.

Martin was born into a family of ministers. His mother's father, A. D. Williams, was the pastor of Ebenezer Baptist Church in Atlanta, Georgia. Martin's father, Martin Sr., was the church's co-pastor. The Williams family and the King family lived together in a comfortable house on Auburn Avenue in Atlanta.

Martin Sr., known to his family as "Daddy King," hadn't always lived in Atlanta. He had grown up on a farm in South Georgia where his father was a sharecropper. A sharecropper

what are civil rights? The rights to freedom and equality given by the US Constitution. African-Americans were often denied their civil rights, especially in the South.

is a farmer who works a small plot of land owned by another farmer. In exchange, he gives the landowner some of his crops at the end of the year. Sharecroppers worked very hard, but they barely made enough money to make ends meet.

The King and Williams families lived in this house in Atlanta, Georgia.

One day, Martin Sr. saw that the landowner, who was white, was cheating the family out of money his father had earned. He told his father about it right in front of the landowner. The landowner was furious. Martin Sr. realized he would have to leave the farm for his own safety and for the safety of his family.

His older sister was living in Atlanta, and he decided to move there, too.

When Martin Sr. moved to Atlanta, he wanted to get an education—but there was a problem.

Atlanta

GEORGIA

There had been no high schools for African-American children in the part of Georgia he was from, so he had only gone to school through the eighth grade. In Atlanta, he started high school at the age of 18, the same age most people graduate.

He worked hard during the day and went to school at night. Sometimes he fell asleep in class, but he didn't give up. Martin Sr. graduated from high school and, later, from Atlanta's Morehouse College.

Atlanta is also where he met and married Alberta Williams, daughter of A. D. Williams. That's when Martin Sr. became co-pastor of Ebenezer Baptist Church and a leader in Atlanta's black community.

Life could be hard for black people in the American South. Segregation kept them separated from white people. Black children

---

what is segregation? Keeping people of different races or religions separate from each other, either by law or by other methods.

and white children went to different schools. Black people had to ride in the back of buses and couldn't play in public parks or swimming pools. Many stores, hotels, and restaurants were for whites only. Even drinking fountains were separated. Worse, black people were paid less than whites for doing the same jobs.

Martin Sr. worked to make life better for people in the black community. He encouraged them to register to vote. He also fought for black teachers to receive the same pay as white teachers.

This is the world that Martin was born into on January 15, 1929. He had an older sister, Christine. He would also have a younger brother,

Alfred Daniel (A. D.). When he was born, Martin was named Michael King just like his father. It wasn't until he was five years old that "Little Mike" became Martin Luther King Jr. His father changed both of their names from Michael to Martin Luther in honor of a famous religious thinker.

Young Martin was like many other boys. He loved his family and was especially close to his grandmother. He liked to play with his friends. He was good at baseball, and he sang in the church choir.

WHAT'S IN A NAME?

Religious thinker Martin Luther worked to change some basic rules of the Christian church in the 1500s. His work led to the separation between the Roman Catholic Church and the new Protestant churches.

One day Martin was impressed by a visiting preacher at the church. "Someday I'm going to have me some big words like that," he told his mother.

Martin had high hopes for himself, but it wasn't long before he began to understand the true meaning of signs that read "Whites only." As he grew older, Martin became more and more aware of segregation and the unfair laws, commonly called Jim Crow laws, that separated him from his dreams. These Jim Crow laws were named after a character in a traveling show. To play this character, a white actor would blacken his face and sing and dance in a way that made fun of black people.

Many white people in the South wanted to make sure African-Americans would not have the same rights as they did. They passed the Jim Crow laws that separated schools, waiting rooms, and restrooms.

The laws also forced black people to ride in the backs of buses and in separate railroad cars—and in almost all cases, the spaces for black people were far worse than those reserved for whites.

The Jim Crow laws made life very difficult for black people in the South. Because the laws also made it nearly impossible for them to register to vote, the African-American community had little hope of being able to change things for the better.

Martin Sr. graduated from Atlanta's Morehouse College.

Here's Martin.

Martin's family poses for a portrait. In the back, from left to right, are Martin's mother, father, and grandmother. That's A. D., Christine, and Martin in the front.

Chapter 2

"Whites only"

Martin's Atlanta neighborhood was almost entirely African-American. As a boy, his parents protected him from racism—until it was time to start school.

Across the street from the King family's home on Auburn Avenue was a store that was owned by a white family. Martin and his brother, A. D., would sometimes play with the storeowner's children. When Martin was six years old, shortly after he and his white friend had started at their separate schools, Martin and A. D. crossed the street to find their playmates.

The boys told Martin and A. D. that they couldn't play with them anymore because they were Negroes.

WORDS MATTER

When Martin was a boy, "Negro" was the polite term used to refer to African-Americans. Many people, however, used the word "colored." Others insulted adult men and women by calling them "boy" or "girl" instead of by their names. There were bigger, uglier insult words, as well. They were used to make black people feel small.

Martin and his brother were confused and sad. When they told their mother what the storeowner's children had said, she was not surprised. Instead, she explained to them why their family didn't go to the movies, eat at nice restaurants, or go to the town's best schools.

Mrs. King taught her children how to get along in the world of Jim Crow laws, but she also made sure that her children knew those laws were unfair and wrong. "You are as good as anyone," she told Martin.

Martin agreed with his mother. He knew the Jim Crow laws weren't right, and he was going to make a difference. "One day I'm going to turn this world upside down," he promised her.

"One day I'm going to turn this world **upside down.**"

Martin Luther King Jr.

Despite his promise, Martin experienced racism again and again. Once when Martin was in a department store with his mother, a white woman suddenly slapped him. She yelled and accused him of stepping on her foot. Martin and his mother could do nothing.

Daddy King drove his own car so he wouldn't have to ride in the back of the bus. One day, a police officer pulled him over and said, "Boy, show me your license." Martin's father pointed to his son and said, "That's a *boy* there. I'm a *man*."

Another time, a shoe-store clerk insisted that Daddy King and Martin move to seats at the back of the store before he would serve them.

What is racism?　　The belief that certain people are better or worse than others because of their race. Hating a group of people because of their race is also racism.

"We'll either buy shoes sitting here, or we won't buy any shoes at all," Daddy King said. They left the store.

When Martin was 14, he traveled to a public-speaking contest with a favorite teacher. Martin's speech, "The Negro and the Constitution," won first prize. In it, he argued that Jim Crow laws were unfair. On the ride home to Atlanta, the bus driver ordered Martin and his teacher to give up their seats to white passengers. Martin was angry, but his teacher convinced him to obey the law. They had to stand for the 90-mile (145-km) trip home. "It was the angriest I have ever been in my life," Martin remembered later.

Despite the racism he experienced, Martin was a successful student. He did extremely well, skipped grades, and finished high school early.

The summer before going to college, Martin accepted a job at a tobacco farm in Connecticut. It was

DID YOU KNOW?

In his speech, Martin said the United States should "give fair play and free opportunity for all people."

Connecticut

Georgia

his first trip north. While there, he saw black and white people working together. He ate at a restaurant and was seated right next to a table of white people. He saw what the world could be like without segregation.

Traveling home on the train, he had to change to a "colored" car when they reached Washington, D.C. When he ate in the train's dining car, he had to sit behind a curtain. Martin started college determined to make things better for African-Americans, especially in the South.

Chapter 3

A clear path

Martin had been a top student in his high school. In fact, his grades were so good that he skipped the twelfth grade.

Because he had skipped another grade when he was younger, he entered Morehouse College in 1944 at just 15 years old.

Morehouse was the same college his father and his grandfather had attended. At first Martin wasn't interested in becoming a minister like the two of them, but he did know that he wanted to serve humanity and the African-American community. He thought he would be able to do that by studying to become a doctor or a lawyer.

In college, Martin joined a group that worked to make black and white people equal in society. He also discovered the work of Henry David Thoreau. Thoreau was a writer who protested slavery and other injustices in the 1800s with civil disobedience. He refused to pay taxes to a government

Henry David Thoreau

he thought was unfair and went to jail for his beliefs. By studying Thoreau, Martin realized non-violent protest could change the world.

At the same time, Martin greatly admired two of his professors, both of whom were ministers. He began to think that by becoming a minister, he could do more good in the world than he could as a doctor or a lawyer.

what is civil disobedience?

When a person uses non-violent, or peaceful, methods when refusing to follow a law they believe to be unjust.

Now Martin had a clear path forward. He would become a Baptist minister and preach about fairness, equality, and peaceful protest.

At 17, Martin gave his first sermon at his father's Ebenezer Baptist Church. Martin started speaking in one of the church's smaller rooms. As he preached, people were drawn to his voice and his message. So many people ended up coming that the sermon had to be moved to the church's main auditorium. It was a very powerful talk. Church members who had watched Martin grow up suddenly saw him as a man instead of a boy.

Daddy King would have been happy for Martin to join him as assistant pastor as soon as he graduated from college, but Martin wanted more education—so at 19, he traveled north to Crozer Theological Seminary in Pennsylvania.

Martin would give many sermons at Ebenezer Baptist Church throughout his life. This picture is of him preaching there in 1960.

At Crozer, Martin was just one of a few black students in a class of about a hundred. Martin knew that some white people, even in the north, had negative images of black people. He made sure to work hard and always be on time to class. He was also always very well dressed. He liked snazzy sports jackets, two-tone shoes, and tweed suits so much that his classmates at Morehouse had given him a nickname—"Tweed."

Martin read the works of many different philosophers, and he began to believe even more strongly in Thoreau's ideas about non-violent protest. He wondered, though, if it would truly be possible to solve all the problems of segregation without resorting to violence.

That changed when Martin discovered the work of Mohandas

Gandhi. Gandhi, an Indian leader, had won his country's freedom from an unfair government, and he had done so using non-violent protest.

Gandhi, Martin wrote in a tribute to him, "resisted with love instead of hate." Martin's study of Gandhi made him believe that he could confront the evils of segregation and racism with the same non-violent methods.

INSPIRING LEADER

Mohandas Gandhi was an Indian activist and leader. He played a big role in helping India gain its independence from Great Britain in the 1930s and 1940s. He also fought for the rights of India's poor. Gandhi's non-violent methods inspired movements for civil rights and freedom around the world. He is often called "Mahatma," a title given to people who are very wise and holy.

Martin graduated from Crozer at the top of his class in 1951 and won a scholarship to continue his studies. Daddy King was so proud of his son that he gave Martin a brand-new green Chevrolet as a graduation gift. Martin drove that car north to Boston, Massachusetts, where he could get his doctoral degree at Boston University.

It was in Boston that he met the woman who would help him change the world— Coretta Scott.

Martin and his sister celebrate their graduations in 1948. Martin graduated from Morehouse College, and Christine graduated from Spelman College.

Chapter 4

Love AND marriage

Even though Martin had moved even farther north, he still found racism in Boston. Fortunately he found Coretta there, too.

"I went into place after place where there were signs that rooms were for rent," Martin later remembered about looking for a home in Boston. "They were for rent until they found out I was a Negro, and suddenly they had just been rented."

Martin eventually found a place to live and focused on his studies. He continued to think about how he could do the most good in the world. He had come to believe that non-violent resistance was the strongest weapon available in the search for civil rights.

But Martin did more than study in Boston. He began to think about finding a wife.

A friend gave Martin the phone number of Coretta Scott, a student at Boston's New England Conservatory of Music. Coretta wanted to be a singer and to teach music. Like Martin, Coretta was from the South—in her case, Alabama.

Coretta Scott

Martin called Coretta and asked her to have lunch with him. At lunch they talked about everything from Southern soul food and music to segregation and racial injustice in the South. From their very first meeting, Martin could tell that Coretta was just as dedicated as he was to the idea of change.

"After an hour, my mind was made up," Martin remembered later. Before lunch was over, he said, "We ought to get married someday."

Daddy King had always wanted Martin to come back to Atlanta, become co-pastor of Ebenezer Baptist Church, and marry an Atlanta girl. He tried to discourage the romance. But the more time Martin spent with Coretta, the more sure he was that he wanted to marry her.

On June 18, 1953, the young couple was married in the front yard of Coretta's family home in Alabama by Daddy King. No hotels in the area would rent a room to black people, so the couple spent their honeymoon night in the guest room of family friends. Those friends just happened to live in a funeral parlor!

Martin and Coretta spent the rest of the summer in Atlanta, and then drove back to Boston to finish their studies.

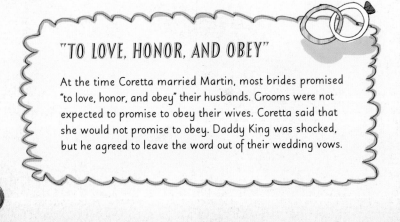

"TO LOVE, HONOR, AND OBEY"

At the time Coretta married Martin, most brides promised "to love, honor, and obey" their husbands. Grooms were not expected to promise to obey their wives. Coretta said that she would not promise to obey. Daddy King was shocked, but he agreed to leave the word out of their wedding vows.

Martin and Coretta smile on their wedding day in 1953.

Martin had a number of choices as to where he would work when he graduated. Three colleges had offered him positions. Two churches in the north wanted him to become their minister. Daddy King hoped Martin and Coretta would come home to Atlanta. Then a church in Montgomery, Alabama—the Dexter Avenue Baptist Church—invited Martin to come down south and preach.

In January 1954, Martin drove from Boston to Montgomery to visit the church. Martin knew that if the church members liked his sermon, he would be asked to become their permanent minister. His sermons were always powerful. They made people think, and they made people want to change the world for the better. The sermon he delivered as a guest preacher that Sunday was no different and, of course, he was offered the job.

Martin and Coretta knew life in the north would be easier for them. Going back down south meant living under Jim Crow

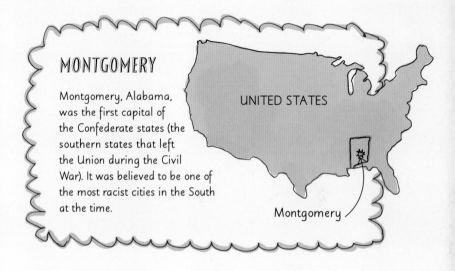

MONTGOMERY

Montgomery, Alabama, was the first capital of the Confederate states (the southern states that left the Union during the Civil War). It was believed to be one of the most racist cities in the South at the time.

UNITED STATES

Montgomery

laws again. It meant having to ride in the back of the bus again. It meant being called names like "boy." But the South was also their home.

Martin and Coretta decided to go where they thought they could do the most good, so they made the hard decision to move to Montgomery. On September 1, 1954, they moved into their new home. They found themselves settling into new jobs, a new house, and a new city all at the same time—and soon they would also find themselves in the middle of a movement to change the world.

5

Rosa Parks REFUSES TO STAND

Martin preached about the need to change the world for the better, and his actions matched his words.

As soon as he moved to Montgomery, Martin joined the Montgomery chapter of the National Association for the Advancement of Colored People (NAACP). He asked the members of

his new church to become members of the NAACP as well. He also told them how important it was that they register to vote. Voting lets people show politicians what they believe in. Martin knew that voting is the way to make changes happen in a community, state, or country.

Martin and Coretta had been in Montgomery for a little more than a year when their first child, a daughter they named Yolanda, was born. Then, just three weeks later, on December 1, 1955, a seamstress named Rosa Parks refused to give up her seat on a Montgomery bus.

Martin, Coretta, and baby Yolanda at home in May 1956.

The bus system in Montgomery was segregated by law. Black people had to sit in the back of the bus while white people sat in the front. If more white passengers got on the bus, black passengers were expected to give up their seats and stand.

TERRIBLE TRICK

Black people had to pay their fares at the front of the bus, then walk around the outside of the bus to the back door. Sometimes white bus drivers would drive off without them after they had paid, just for fun.

Rosa Parks

Rosa, who had been a secretary for the NAACP, decided she had had enough. One night after work, a bus driver ordered her to give up her seat for a white man. She refused, and was arrested.

Martin held a meeting with Montgomery's black civic leaders and the ministers at his church. They agreed it was time to protest their unfair treatment with a bus boycott. They worked all weekend to get the word out to the black community.

On Monday, December 5, Martin and Coretta got up early to watch the first bus drive past the stop in front of their house. There was not one person on that normally crowded bus!

What is a boycott? When people refuse to deal with a person or an organization as a way of protesting.

Martin drove around the city to see what was happening. Men and women walked to work. Students walked to school. The sidewalks were crowded, but the buses were empty.

The first day of the boycott was a huge success. That night black leaders formed the Montgomery Improvement Association to lead the boycott. They made Martin their president.

City leaders were unhappy. They ordered taxis to charge higher fares to try to force people back on the buses. The community organized carpools instead, and then the city tried to put a stop to them, too. Martin urged everyone to stay strong and remember their protest was non-violent. He got hate mail and nasty phone calls from the Ku Klux Klan (KKK), but he didn't back down.

One night, Martin was at a meeting when someone threw a firebomb onto his front porch. He rushed home to make sure Coretta and Yolanda were safe. Luckily they had been in the back of the house. People gathered around the house. They were angry, and they

HATEFUL GROUP

The Ku Klux Klan, or KKK, is a hate group. The KKK was formed after the Civil War and was active in almost every southern state. Its members used violence and murder to frighten black people and to keep them from taking leading roles in society.

wanted justice. Martin knew
things could quickly become
out of control.

He walked out onto
the porch, held up his
hand for silence, and
began to speak. "We
must meet hate with
love," he told the
crowd, and he asked
them to keep faith that
the boycott would work.
His inspiring words
prevented what could
have turned into a riot.

"We must meet **hate** with love."

Martin Luther King Jr., 1956

When Montgomery's government declared the bus boycott illegal, its organizers weren't intimidated or scared. People began showing up at the jail, turning themselves in for boycotting.

Television news cameras were filming when Martin left the courtroom where he was convicted of violating the law and ordered to pay a $500 fine. Suddenly, Martin and the boycott were national news.

While all of this was happening, Martin and the Montgomery Improvement Association brought their case to the US Supreme Court.

What is the Supreme Court?

The highest court in the United States. It is one of the three branches of government established by the US Constitution.

On November 15, 1956, nearly a full year after the boycott had begun, the US Supreme Court declared that the laws forcing black passengers to ride in the back of the bus were unconstitutional.

A few weeks later, on December 21, 1956, integrated buses began running. Martin waited at the bus stop in front of his house, and when the bus came, he got on and rode in the front seat. The Montgomery bus boycott had ended in success, and a new freedom movement was born. Martin would soon be called upon to be its leader.

African-Americans in Montgomery walk to work during the bus boycott. They disapproved of the unfair laws.

After the Supreme Court's ruling, Martin waits with friends to board a newly desegregated bus.

Here's Rosa.

Rosa Parks is one of the first people onto the bus after the boycott is over. What began with her refusal to give up her seat had ended in success.

Chapter 6

THE movement SPREADS

Integrating the buses in Montgomery had been a success. The boycott brought national attention to Martin and his cause.

Martin and other black ministers met in Atlanta to talk about next steps. They decided to form an organization—the Southern Christian Leadership Conference, or SCLC—dedicated to integration and the fight for civil rights. Martin was named their chairman. He traveled around the country giving speeches, and he even made the cover of *Time* magazine in February 1957.

While Martin was traveling around the country, Coretta was often at home alone

What is integration?

Bringing people from different races together to make sure that they have equal rights.

with Yolanda, and later with Martin Luther King III, who was born in October 1957.

Over the next two years, people in the South worked to integrate schools. In the 1954 case of Brown v. Board of Education, the Supreme Court had ruled that segregated schools were unequal and against the law. Despite the ruling, many white southerners still had a one-word answer to the idea of integrated schools: "Never!"

COURAGEOUS STUDENTS

In 1957, nine black students enrolled in Little Rock Central High School in Little Rock, Arkansas. On their first day, the students were met with angry white protestors, and the governor of Arkansas wouldn't allow them in. President Eisenhower sent soldiers to make sure the students could enter the school. The soldiers guarded them for the entire school year, but they couldn't protect them from the ugly things white students said. It was the start of a long, painful process of integrating schools in the South.

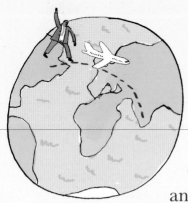

Martin knew the fight for integration would be a long one, and he wanted to learn even more about non-violent protest in order to win it. In 1959, he and Coretta traveled to India. They walked in the footsteps of Gandhi and came home believing even more strongly in peaceful protest.

The demands of the freedom movement made it impossible for Martin to be a full-time pastor in Montgomery. After returning from India, the family moved to Atlanta, where Martin would share duties with Daddy King at Ebenezer Baptist Church.

Black students in the South had been holding non-violent protests of their own. They said it was unfair that they could shop in stores, but that those same stores wouldn't serve them at their lunch counters. On February 1, 1960, four college students in Greensboro, North Carolina, sat down at a Woolworth lunch

Woolworth department store lunch counter, Greensboro.

counter and tried to order. "We don't serve colored here," they were told. The men sat quietly until the store closed. The next day, even more students showed up.

In cities across the South, college students held sit-ins at lunch counters, movie theaters, and parks. They were yelled at, beaten, and had food thrown at them, but the students didn't react. Instead, they formed the Student Nonviolent Coordinating Committee (SNCC).

What is a sit-in?   A protest in which people sit in one place and refuse to leave until they are forced to, or given what they demand.

Martin is handcuffed and brought to the courthouse after his arrest in 1960.

In October 1960, the SNCC asked Martin to join a protest in Atlanta. Martin walked into the department store and sat at the "Whites only" lunch counter. He and 75 students were arrested for trespassing. Five days later, they were released from jail after the store owners dropped the charges—but Martin was arrested again on a fake traffic violation and sentenced to four months in Georgia State Prison.

Martin's supporters contacted the two men who were running for president at the time, John F. Kennedy and Richard M. Nixon. Nixon made no comment, but Kennedy called Coretta and said he would do what he could. Soon Martin was released on bail.

On the Sunday before Election Day, black ministers across the country spoke out in favor of Kennedy. In one of the closest elections in United States history, Kennedy won the presidency.

John F. Kennedy

DID YOU KNOW?

The Woolworth lunch counter where the students held their first sit-in is now at the Smithsonian Museum of American History in Washington, D.C.

The student sit-ins at lunch counters had been successful. Store owners lost so much business that they agreed to serve black people alongside white people. However, many other places were still segregated. Martin met with the new President Kennedy and his brother, Attorney General Robert F. Kennedy, to talk about a civil rights bill to end segregation in the United States once and for all.

The civil rights bill was on a long list of things Kennedy wanted to do, but it wasn't too high on that list. As the Kings welcomed their third child, Dexter, in January 1961, Martin thought about how to get President Kennedy to pay attention.

People wait at a segregated lunch counter in 1960. Sit-ins and "stand-in-line" protests forced businesses to reconsider their rules.

A "stand-in-line" protest takes place at a movie theater in Nashville, Tennessee. About 300 people protested at Nashville movie theaters in 1961 by waiting in line and refusing to leave.

7

"Letter FROM BIRMINGHAM JAIL"

The Civil Rights Movement had made great progress by 1961, but there was still a long way to go.

A group of black and white students called Freedom Riders decided to travel south to test a federal law that said places like bus and train stations could no longer be segregated. On their trip down, one of their buses was firebombed outside Birmingham, Alabama. When the riders ran off the bus, the attackers beat them with baseball bats and chains. More students arrived to keep the Freedom Rides going. Their protests were peaceful, but they were often met with violence and arrests.

Martin flew to Montgomery to talk to a group of Freedom Riders. An angry mob threw rocks and tear gas around the church where they were meeting. Martin got in touch with Robert F. Kennedy, who sent soldiers from the National Guard to protect the Freedom Riders and their supporters.

One city that refused to give up its "Whites only" waiting room was Albany, Georgia. When SNCC students tried to make the train station end its segregation policy, they were thrown in jail. In response, Martin organized and led a

National Guard soldiers come to Alabama to help protect the Freedom Riders on May 22, 1961.

peaceful protest march through the city singing "We Shall Overcome." He was arrested. More people protested. More people were put in jail.

One night, a woman was beaten when she tried to bring food to the jail. The black community couldn't hold in its anger, and a riot broke out. Martin left the city. He felt as if his time in Albany had been a failure.

A SONG TO INSPIRE

"We Shall Overcome" is a gospel song dating from the early 1900s. In the 1950s, the song was discovered by the members of the Civil Rights Movement and became their anthem. "We Shall Overcome" was sung on protest marches and in sit-ins. Protesters were beaten and kept singing. They were hauled off to jail and kept singing. The words brought courage when the protesters needed it the most.

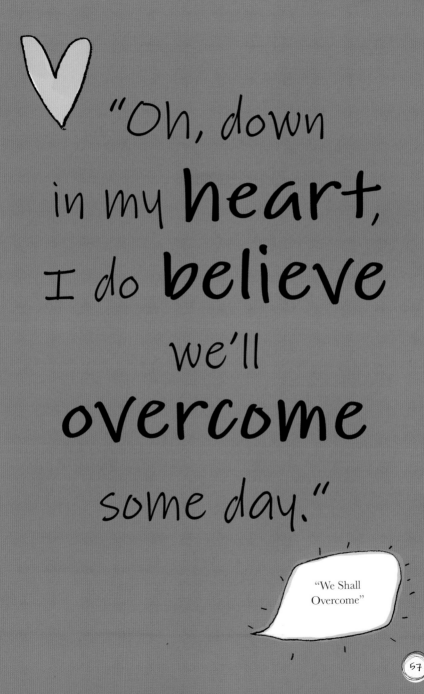

"Oh, down in my **heart,** I do **believe** we'll **overcome** some day."

"We Shall Overcome"

When Bernice was born in 1963, Martin's family was complete. This family portrait of Martin, Coretta, and their four children was taken four years later, in 1967.

Martin was thinking about the next moves for the freedom movement when his fourth child, Bernice, was born in 1963. After some time at home with his family, he and the other SCLC leaders decided to make the city of Birmingham, Alabama, their focus.

Birmingham's Commissioner for Public Safety, Eugene "Bull" Connor, had done nothing while Freedom Riders were bombed and beaten. He was against the Civil Rights Movement and had no interest in helping anyone fighting for equality. To combat this, the SCLC launched Project C. The C was for "confrontation."

Project C targeted "Whites only" lunch counters at three stores in the city. Black students sat at the counters and refused to move. Twenty-one people were arrested the very first day. The next day, more members of Martin's "non-violent army" arrived to take their places—and the next day and the next. In all, hundreds were arrested. Store owners were upset about the business they were losing.

A state court ordered an end to the demonstrations. Instead, Martin led a march. He was arrested and thrown in jail.

Martin was kept in solitary confinement, meaning he was isolated from the other

what is confrontation?

A meeting in which people challenge, or confront, one another, usually in an angry way.

prisoners. He wasn't even allowed anything to read, but a friend smuggled in a newspaper. In the newspaper, he read that white ministers were asking him to stop his protest. Martin's lawyers smuggled a pen into the jail for him, and with that pen, he wrote something that would become famous: his "Letter from Birmingham Jail."

When he was released, Martin saw protestors were getting discouraged. Many were still in jail.

"LETTER FROM BIRMINGHAM JAIL"

Some white ministers in Birmingham asked the black community not to support the SCLC's efforts. From his cell, Martin wrote a letter that would be published in newspapers across the country. He defended the non-violent demonstrations as a necessary step to create change. "We will reach the goal of freedom in Birmingham and all over the nation, because the goal of America is freedom," he wrote.

Young protestors show their support for integration during the Children's Crusade. They knew they would likely be arrested.

Others needed to work to feed their families. The movement turned to a new source of protesters—children. On May 2, 1963, the Children's Crusade began. More than 1,000 college, high school, and even elementary school students began a march from the 16th Street Baptist Church. Many were arrested. The next day, more arrived to take their place.

Bull Connor demanded the students turn back. They refused, so he told his police and firefighters to let the children have it. Police dogs lunged at them, and firefighters turned their powerful water hoses on them. News cameras captured it all.

Day after day, the children kept coming. Finally, the firefighters refused to attack them anymore. They were impressed by the children's bravery.

On May 10, 1963—38 days after Project C began—an agreement was reached with the city's businesses. They could hold out no longer. Integration would finally come to Birmingham.

That night, a bomb exploded outside of Martin's hotel room. He had already left the city and was unharmed, but he returned to Birmingham to stop the riots that broke out.

The riots made President Kennedy see that a civil rights bill was needed. He urged Congress to get to work. Martin and the other leaders wanted to make sure Congress listened. They planned a march on Washington, D.C., to show the world how much they needed freedom.

"It ought to be possible ... for every **American** to enjoy the **privileges** of being American **without** regard to his **race** or his **color**."

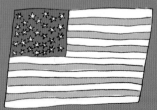

John F. Kennedy,
June 11, 1963

8

"I have a **dream**"

**The night President Kennedy told Congress
a civil rights bill was long overdue, a black
leader named Medgar Evers was shot and killed.**

The shooting took place in Jackson, the capital
city of Mississippi. The shooter was a white
supremacist, which is a person who believes
that white people are better than black people
and all other races.

MEDGAR EVERS

Evers wasn't allowed to vote when he came
home from World War II. In response, he
organized local chapters of the NAACP
and traveled all over Mississippi to lead
voter registration drives. In Jackson, he
fought to end segregation and to open
up good jobs to African-Americans.

The black community was sad and angry. Martin was sad and angry, too. He knew that he would have to keep the pressure on Congress to make sure a civil rights bill was passed. He and the SCLC planned a march to prove just how many people supported equal rights for African-Americans.

More than 250,000 people of all different races traveled from every state in the nation to participate in the March on Washington for Jobs and Freedom on August 28, 1963. They traveled by car and bus. They traveled by plane. A few even walked all the way from New York City. People came to show their government and the rest of the country that the Jim Crow laws had to go.

Many government leaders, including Robert F. Kennedy, said they feared that there would be violence. The protestors proved them wrong. They peacefully marched from the Washington Monument to the Lincoln Memorial, singing "We Shall Overcome" all the way. When they arrived at the Lincoln Memorial, the crowd gathered to hear speeches.

WE MARCH FOR JOBS!

END SEGREGATED RULES IN PUBLIC SCHOOLS.

WE DEMAND JOBS!

I.U.E ALF-CIO FOR FULL EMPLOYMENT

for freedom

WE MARCH FOR JOBS FOR ALL NOW!

Religious leaders and members of different civil rights groups gave inspiring speeches, and well-known singers such as Marian Anderson, Joan Baez, and Bob Dylan led everyone in the national anthem and other songs. However, it was Martin's speech that meant the most to the crowd. It has since been named one of the greatest speeches in American history.

Martin told the marchers that he had a dream. He described a world in which people of all colors were not only equal, but also loved one another. He shared a dream of the sons of former slaves and the sons of former slave owners sitting down together at the table of brotherhood.

"I have a dream that my four little children will one day live in a nation where they will not be judged by the color of their skin but by the content of their character. I have a dream today!"

He finished by saying that only when the country "let freedom ring," from every state, city, village, and hamlet, would people truly be free.

The march and especially Martin's speech made national news. His words inspired the entire country and even the world. It was one of the greatest moments of the Civil Rights Movement, and people everywhere were optimistic that freedom and equality would surely follow.

Martin addresses the large crowd gathered to hear his speech at the 1963 March on Washington.

Just two weeks later, on September 15, 1963, Martin was preaching his Sunday sermon at the Ebenezer Baptist Church when he learned that a bomb had gone off in Birmingham.

Four members of the Ku Klux Klan had set off sticks of dynamite at the 16th Street Baptist Church, the church that had been a gathering place for marchers during the Birmingham protests earlier that year. Twenty-two people were injured in the terrible attack. Even worse, three 14-year-old girls and one 11-year-old girl who had been attending Sunday school that day were killed.

The 16th Street Baptist Church is still an active church. It was named a National Historic Landmark in 2006.

Martin flew to Birmingham to try to keep riots from breaking out, but the murder of four young girls made many people wonder if non-violence was still the way to go. Some believed that it was time to start fighting for their rights with the same violent tactics that were being used against them. Martin urged his followers to continue to be peaceful. He never stopped believing that non-violence was the only way to change the world.

Violence shook the country again on the afternoon of November 22, 1963. President Kennedy was shot and killed in Dallas, Texas. Martin was sad to lose the man who had been a friend to the Civil Rights Movement and to Martin himself.

With Kennedy's death, his vice president— Lyndon B. Johnson—became the new president of the United States.

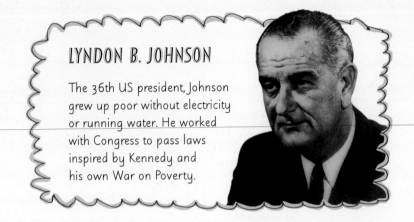

LYNDON B. JOHNSON

The 36th US president, Johnson grew up poor without electricity or running water. He worked with Congress to pass laws inspired by Kennedy and his own War on Poverty.

Five days later, President Johnson spoke to Congress. In his speech, he said that the best way to honor President Kennedy's memory was to pass the Civil Rights Bill.

On July 2, 1964, Martin was standing behind President Johnson when he signed the Civil Rights Act. The act made discrimination in public places and businesses illegal. It also made it possible for the government to force public schools to end segregation.

It was a step forward for civil rights. Making sure black people had the right to vote, however, was something that Martin would have to continue fighting for.

Martin looks on as President Johnson signs the Civil Rights Act of 1964.

Chapter 9

Selma

The March on Washington and the passing of the Civil Rights Act of 1964 were victories for Martin and African-Americans all over the country.

Martin's strong words had inspired many people. At the end of the year, he discovered that he was the winner of the Nobel Peace Prize. In his acceptance speech, he announced that he would share the prize and the prize money with the Civil Rights Movement. "I still believe that we shall overcome," he declared. "This faith can give us courage to face the uncertainties of the future."

What is the Nobel Peace Prize?

A medal given each year to a person or group who has worked for world peace. Nobel prizes are also given for chemistry, physics, medicine, and literature.

FREEDOM SUMMER

During the summer of 1964, thousands of northern college students, many of them white, went down south to encourage African-Americans to register to vote. The students also set up Freedom Schools to prepare voters for the difficult tests they would have to pass in order to register. The students were often beaten and jailed for their efforts. Three of them were killed by the KKK in Mississippi.

Throughout 1964 the Student Nonviolent Coordinating Committee (SNCC) had been working in Selma, Alabama, to register black voters with little success. Part of the problem was that a state judge had made it illegal for black people to hold group meetings. Another part of the problem was the local sheriff, Jim Clark. He said that any black person who tried to vote would be beaten with clubs and cattle prods. The city's black leaders turned to Martin and the SCLC for help. Martin answered their call and arrived in Selma in January 1965.

On January 18, 1965, 50 African-Americans marched as a group to the courthouse to register to vote. They were arrested. Over and over again, more people marched to the courthouse only to be arrested. Each time, Sheriff Clark met the groups wearing a pin on his uniform that read, "Never."

On February 1, Martin gathered 700 supporters and marched to the courthouse. He was arrested and thrown in jail, which made headlines all across the country.

More and more people kept marching in Selma and in other counties in Alabama, too. A group of 105 black teachers marched, even though they knew that their white school board might fire them for doing so. In another march, a young man was shot and killed by a state trooper while he was trying to protect his mother from being beaten.

People dance during the civil rights protests in Selma. They also marched and chanted to show their support for voting rights.

Protesters link arms and sing outside the Dallas Country Courthouse in Selma. Many of them were later arrested.

MALCOLM X

Malcolm X, a black leader and powerful speaker, disagreed with Martin's belief in non-violence. He thought they should be fighting violence with violence. He urged African-Americans to be proud of their heritage, and instead of integration, he wanted the races to be separate. Despite their differences, Martin and Malcolm X respected each other. Martin was deeply sad when Malcolm X was killed in 1965.

While Martin was in jail, the SNCC invited Malcolm X to speak in Selma. Malcolm X and Martin had very different views, and Martin was afraid the people would turn to violence. He organized a peaceful march as a way to make sure that wouldn't happen.

The march would begin in Selma and end in Montgomery, a 54-mile (87-km) walk that would show the nation that African-Americans in the South needed voting rights, and they needed them now. Alabama's governor, George Wallace, said the march could not take place.

Martin was preaching in Atlanta on March 7, 1965, when 600 people gathered to begin their march. As they crossed over the Edmund Pettus Bridge, Alabama state troopers were waiting. The marchers were met with violence and tear gas. The news coverage shocked the nation. More than 70 marchers had to be hospitalized, and many more had minor injuries. The day came to be known as Bloody Sunday.

Protesters encounter the waiting Alabama state troopers on their march from Selma to Montgomery in 1965.

Martin asked religious leaders to support the marchers. People from all over the country came to Selma, including white ministers, priests, and rabbis. They gathered to march again a few days later, but a federal judge had banned their protest. Although Martin had never ignored a federal court order, he felt the need to gather anyway—"because our nation has a date with destiny," he said.

When they reached the bridge and were ordered to stop, Martin and the others knelt to pray. Then they turned around and went back to Selma until they could be heard by a federal judge and given permission to march.

That night, three white ministers were walking home from dinner when they were beaten by members of the KKK. One of the ministers, James Reeb, was killed.

There was a national uproar. President Johnson addressed Congress on television and asked for a voting rights bill.

A federal judge ruled that the people had the constitutional right to march from Selma to Montgomery. On Sunday, March 21, more than 3,000 people gathered. They were protected from violence by the National Guard. By the time they reached Montgomery five days later, their number had increased to 25,000 people.

On August 6, 1965, President Johnson signed the Voting Rights Act. This new law banned the difficult tests and other means the southern states had been using to keep black people from voting. By the following summer, 9,000 African-Americans were registered to vote in Selma.

Holding hands, Martin and Coretta lead more than 3,000 marchers across the Edmund Pettis Bridge in Selma. The five-day voting rights march to the capital in Montgomery proved to the world that peaceful protest could win the day.

Chapter **10**

THE **poverty** PROBLEM

By 1965, 10 years after the Montgomery bus boycott, the Civil Rights Movement had seen many successes.

Black people could vote. They could sit anywhere they wanted to on buses and eat at any lunch counter. However, many lived in crime-filled slums and still didn't have good jobs. Inner-city schools were often falling apart and didn't have enough teachers. Frustrated children dropped out of high school, giving them little hope for a better future. Despite the Civil Rights Movement's successes, black people were struggling, and the cause of their struggles was poverty.

What is a slum? A poor, crowded, and dirty section of a city. A slum in which people of one race or religious group live is called a ghetto.

This was true of African-Americans all over the country, not just in the south. Cities like New York, Los Angeles, and Chicago were among the worst.

In August 1965, the same month the Voting Rights Act was signed, angry and frustrated people started a riot in the black neighborhood of Watts in Los Angeles, California. A black man had been arrested by white police officers for what the crowd believed was a made-up traffic charge. The riot lasted for six days and led to riots in other cities. Martin began to see that as long as black people lived in poverty, both in the north as well as in the south, they could never be truly free.

Martin and his fellow marchers link arms to show unity as they march to Chicago's City Hall in July 1965.

The riots in Los Angeles and other cities convinced Martin that he had to do more to fight poverty. Martin visited slums in New York City and Massachusetts. In July 1965, he was asked to lead a march in Chicago from the black ghetto to City Hall. He saw that most black people living in the city were poor with low-paying jobs or no jobs at all. There were laws against segregation, but that didn't stop white landlords from refusing to rent houses and apartments to black families.

In 1966, Martin, Coretta, and their four children moved to Chicago. Martin felt that he needed to live among the people he was trying to help. They lived in a run-down, two-bedroom apartment in a black neighborhood. There were no parks nearby for the children to play in. Their rent was $90 a month. A nicer apartment in a poor white neighborhood cost $10 less, but most of the white landlords there wouldn't have rented to the King family.

Martin criticized Chicago's white leaders, especially Mayor Richard Daley, for not doing enough to help Chicago's poor.

Richard J. Daley

Mayor Daley wasn't happy with Martin's attention. He had tried to keep Chicago's black residents on his side with weak promises to clean up the ghettos, but the community was restless. They wanted change, and they weren't ready to commit to non-violence.

Daley was the mayor of Chicago from 1955 until he died in 1976. He was considered to be the last of the big-city "bosses," mayors who kept a tight control on their cities by giving government jobs to their supporters. Daley was powerful, but he did little to end segregation.

Soon Martin realized the movement faced an even bigger problem. President Johnson was turning his attention to the Vietnam War.

Antiwar protests were taking place all over the United States. The Civil Rights Movement was being pushed aside in the face of these other worries.

Young leaders in the movement had very different views about its future. Some of them carried guns. They thought it might be time to fight back against beatings at the hands of white police officers. Martin believed they were wrong. He never stopped believing that peaceful resistance was better and more effective than violence.

He worried that young black men who had few opportunities at home were being sent thousands of miles away to Vietnam to fight for the rights of others. He spoke out against the war, something that made President Johnson unhappy. Many years before, President Kennedy had warned Martin that the FBI was keeping an eye on him. Now they were watching him even more closely.

With violence at home on the rise and attention in Congress turned to the war, Martin tried to keep his non-violent movement in people's minds. In 1967, he published a new book called *Where Do We Go From Here: Chaos or Community?* In it, he urged people of all races to work together to bring an end to racism and poverty. Unless everyone participated in the movement, he argued, true change would never come.

After the book was published, Martin decided to stage another march on the nation's capital in the spring of 1968. He wanted to bring people of all races together to demonstrate for better jobs and higher pay. Martin called this project the Poor People's Campaign.

"No **great** victories victories are **won** in a war for the **transformation** of a whole people without **total** participation."

Martin Luther King Jr.,
*Where Do We Go From Here:
Chaos or Community?*, 1967

11

"**Free** at last"

Martin was busy organizing his Poor People's Campaign in Chicago when he got an urgent call for help.

Black sanitation workers in Memphis, Tennessee, were on strike. They had started a union, which is an organized group of workers. The union had been trying to get better working conditions and fair pay for its members. The city leaders had said no.

The strikers marched every day wearing signs that read, "I AM A MAN." They wanted respect, and they wanted fairness. Instead, they were beaten by police. Then the city got a judge to order the marches to stop.

What is a strike? When workers refuse to work in order to convince or force their employer to meet their demands.

Memphis sanitation workers go on strike to protest unfair working conditions and pay in 1968.

People were getting angry. Strike organizers worried that violence would break out. They asked Martin to come and speak. His staff urged him to stay focused on the Poor People's Campaign, but Martin couldn't say no to the black workers' call for help. He arrived in Memphis on March 18, 1968, and checked into the Lorraine Motel.

That night, Martin spoke at a rally in front of 17,000 people. He encouraged the strikers to stick together and keep going.

Today, the former Lorraine Motel in downtown Memphis is part of the National Civil Rights Museum.

He knew that they had to keep marching until they won their case.

Another protest march was scheduled, and Martin decided to lead it. More than 6,000 people were waiting for him to lead them to City Hall on March 28. Martin sensed some tension in the crowd, but he had no idea that some young men were determined to get violent. He was waving to some fans when he heard the sound of breaking glass. Behind Martin, teenagers were smashing store windows and stealing what they found inside. In front of Martin, police waited in full riot gear.

Martin had said he would never lead a violent march, and he immediately called it off. People did their best to get away from the scene while police fired tear gas and guns. By the time it was all over, 155 stores were damaged, 60 people were injured, and one teenager was killed.

The violence made the national news. Martin was horrified. He couldn't stop thinking about the boy who had been killed. He knew he couldn't let the violent forces in the black community take over. He wanted to prove that a non-violent march was possible. This next march, he promised, would be better organized, and it would be peaceful.

On April 3, Martin was back at the Lorraine Motel. He had received death threats. Someone had even said there was a bomb on his plane, but Martin persisted. That night, he spoke to a crowd of 2,000 people. Newspaper reporters and television cameras were there to record his speech.

Martin spoke without a script. He talked about the threats to his own life, but said that he wasn't afraid. He believed that he was doing

God's work. He knew there were difficult days
ahead, but he believed they'd win in the end.

"And I may not get there with you," he said
to the crowd. "But I want you to know tonight
that we as a people will get to the Promised
Land. So I'm happy tonight. I'm not
worried about anything. I'm not
fearing any man. Mine eyes
have seen the glory
of the coming of
the Lord."

He finished his speech with the words of one of his favorite Negro spirituals: "Free at last! Free at last! Thank God almighty we are free at last." Martin's speech was a huge success. It was televised all over the country.

He spent the next day, April 4, organizing the march with his staff at the Lorraine Motel. They were getting ready to go out to dinner when Martin stepped out onto the balcony of his room, room 306. In an instant, he was struck by a bullet from a high-powered rifle. He was rushed to the hospital, but it was too late. Dr. Martin Luther King Jr. was dead.

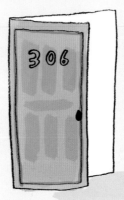

"I want
you to know
tonight that
we as a people
will get to the
Promised Land."

Martin Luther
King Jr.,
April 3, 1968

Chapter 12

A lasting **legacy**

The loss of Martin was felt all over the world. His words and deeds have lived on, and his influence can still be felt today.

Coretta was on her way to the Atlanta airport when she learned Martin had been assassinated, or killed. She turned around and went home to comfort her children.

Soon the details of Martin's assassin were discovered. James Earl Ray was a racist and a criminal. He escaped from a Missouri prison in 1967 and spent the next year traveling in Canada, Mexico, and the United States. When he read about Martin's plans in Memphis, he had traveled there and waited. He shot

James Earl Ray

Martin from the window of a house near the Lorraine Motel, then fled the country. He was arrested in London, England, two months later. Ray confessed to the crime and was sentenced to 99 years in prison.

President Johnson announced that Sunday, April 7, would be a national day of mourning. Flags were lowered to half mast around the country. Leaders from all over the world spoke out about Martin's life, and thousands of Americans marched, prayed, and sang songs in his honor. Most of the mourning was peaceful, but some black communities erupted in anger and violence.

SHOWING RESPECT

A flag flying at half mast, or half staff, is seen as a sign of respect and mourning in many countries around the world, including the United States.

Coretta knew Martin's work was far from finished. Days after his death, she and her children led protesters in a quiet, peaceful march in Memphis. A week later, the city recognized the sanitation workers' union and agreed to give the workers fair pay.

On April 9, Martin was buried in Atlanta. The burial took place after a service at the Ebenezer Baptist Church, the same church that he had grown up in. His gravestone is inscribed with the words he loved: "Free

at last. Free at last. Thank God Almighty I'm Free at last."

Coretta and their four children continued to carry his message and fight to make Martin's dream a reality, in the United States as well as in the rest of the world. So did many of Martin's followers.

On April 9, 1968, four days after Martin's death, Coretta leads a march for the sanitation workers' union in Memphis.

Protesters wearing signs that say "Honor King: End Racism!" march through the streets to show their support for equal rights.

Today Martin and his teachings are studied by people all over the world. Parks, schools, and streets are named after him. In 1980, Martin's home on Auburn Avenue in Atlanta, the Ebenezer Baptist Church, and his burial site were named a National Historic Landmark. The nearby Martin Luther King Jr. Center for Nonviolent Social Change, which Coretta helped create in 1968, develops leaders who follow Martin's principles of non-violence as a way to make the world a better place.

In April 2016, the United States Treasury Department announced that Martin may one day join former president Abraham Lincoln on the five-dollar bill, to honor his 1963 "I Have a Dream" speech at the Lincoln Memorial.

Coretta campaigned for January 15, Martin's

What is a National Historic Landmark? A place the government has recognized as extremely important to US history.

birthday, to be named a national holiday. It took many years and many meetings with politicians, but Coretta didn't give up. Finally, a bill sponsored by Senator Ted Kennedy, the younger brother of President Kennedy, was signed into law in 1983. The first Martin Luther King Jr. Day was celebrated in January 1986. People now celebrate the holiday in the United States on the third Monday in January.

A LIFE OF ACTIVISM

Coretta was an activist for equality and civil rights until her death in 2006. She is also remembered for promoting children's books. In 1969, the American Library Association began awarding the Coretta Scott King Book Awards to African-American writers and illustrators of the best books for children. Winners continue to be announced every January.

A display at the National Civil Rights Museum in Memphis honors the Montgomery bus boycott of 1955–1956.

Across the country, museums dedicated to preserving Martin's teachings and telling the story of the Civil Rights Movement continue to help keep his legacy alive. More than 300,000 visitors come to the National Civil Rights Museum in Memphis each year, and the Civil Rights Memorial in Montgomery honors the martyrs of the movement— including Martin.

What is a martyr?   A person whose death inspires others to fight for their cause.

In 2016, the National Museum of African American History and Culture opened in Washington, D.C. The museum documents African-American life, art, history, and culture from the times of slavery to the present day. It often has special exhibits and celebrations in memory of Martin.

America has made some advances over the years, but the country continues to struggle

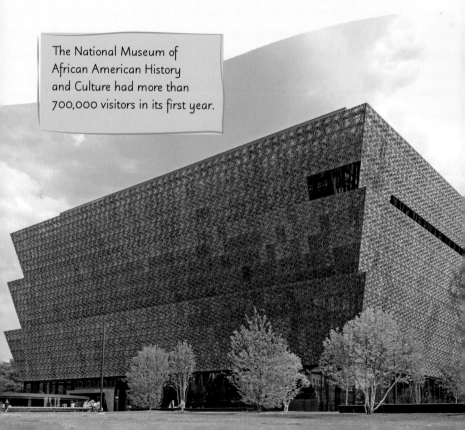

The National Museum of African American History and Culture had more than 700,000 visitors in its first year.

with some of the same problems Martin
had tried to solve. Laws have been passed,
and passionate people continue to fight for
equality for all races. However, many African-
Americans still live in ghettos and don't have
the same educational opportunities as white
people. Martin's dream may have not yet come
true, but his words continue to inspire people
everywhere who want to make the world a
better place.

Martin's
family tree

Martin Luther
King Jr.

1929-1968

Martin's first child,
Yolanda, was an
actor, producer,
and public speaker.

Daughter

Yolanda
Denise King
1955-2007

Father

Martin Luther
King Sr.
1899–1984

Mother

Alberta
Williams King
1904–1974

Sister

Christine
King Farris
1927–

Brother

Alfred Daniel
Williams King
1930–1969

Wife

Coretta Scott
King
1927–2006

Martin
married
Coretta
in 1953.

Martin
Luther
King III
1957–

Son

Dexter
Scott King
1961–

Son

Bernice
Albertine
King
1963–

Daughter

111

Timeline

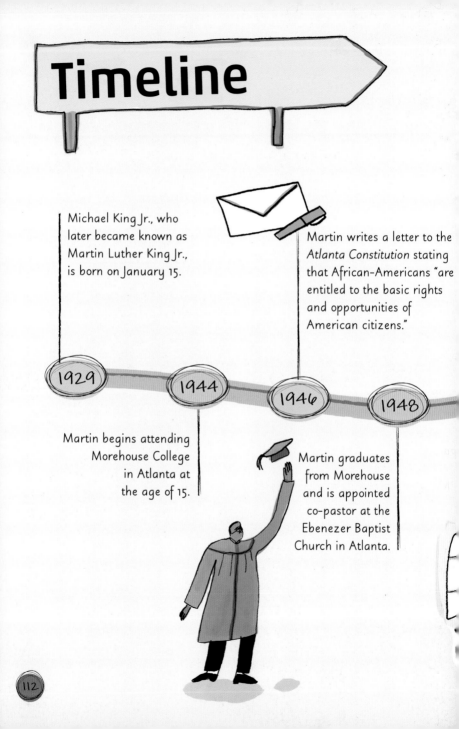

Michael King Jr., who later became known as Martin Luther King Jr., is born on January 15.

Martin writes a letter to the *Atlanta Constitution* stating that African-Americans "are entitled to the basic rights and opportunities of American citizens."

1929

1944

1946

1948

Martin begins attending Morehouse College in Atlanta at the age of 15.

Martin graduates from Morehouse and is appointed co-pastor at the Ebenezer Baptist Church in Atlanta.

Martin marries Coretta at the Scott family home near Marion, Alabama.

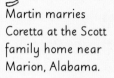

Activist Rosa Parks is arrested for refusing to give up her seat on a city bus to a white person. The Montgomery bus boycott begins.

1953   1954   1955   1956

Martin becomes the pastor of Dexter Avenue Baptist Church in Montgomery, Alabama.

The Montgomery bus boycott ends. Martin is one of the first passengers to board the newly integrated buses.

In January, Southern black ministers meet in Atlanta to discuss how to fight against segregation. They create the Southern Christian Leadership Conference (SCLC) and name Martin its chairman.

The Civil Rights Act is signed. In the same year, Martin receives the Nobel Peace Prize.

In October, Martin is arrested after participating in a sit-in in Atlanta.

1957

1960

1963

1964

In May, at the Lincoln Memorial in Washington, D.C., Martin delivers his "Give Us the Ballot" speech.

The March on Washington draws more than 200,000 people to the Lincoln Memorial. Martin delivers his "I Have a Dream" speech.

WE MARCH WITH SELMA

In March, Martin helps lead the five-day march from Selma to Montgomery in Alabama. In August, President Johnson signs the Voting Rights Act.

Martin is assassinated at the Lorraine Motel in Memphis, Tennessee.

1965

1967

1968

Martin announces his plan to organize the Poor People's Campaign in Washington, D.C.

Quiz

1 In what year was Martin born?

2 How old was Martin when he won first prize at a public-speaking contest?

3 Who was the inspiring leader whose work made Martin believe in non-violent protest?

4 To which southern city did Martin and Coretta move in September 1954?

5 What do the letters in NAACP stand for?

6 On the cover of which magazine did Martin appear in February 1957?

7 On what two materials did Martin write his "Letter from Birmingham Jail"?

Do you remember what you've read? How many of these questions about Martin's life can you answer?

 What 1964 act made discrimination in public places and businesses illegal?

 What major award did Martin win in 1964?

 Who was the mayor of Chicago when Martin and his family moved there in 1966?

 What phrase was on the sanitation workers' signs during their strike in 1968?

 In which month are the Coretta Scott King Book Awards announced each year?

Answers on page 128

Who's who?

Anderson, Marian
(1897–1993) singer who performed at the March on Washington

Baez, Joan
(1941–) musician who performed at the March on Washington

Connor, Eugene "Bull"
(1897–1973) Commissioner of Public Safety in Birmingham, Alabama, who opposed the Civil Rights Movement

Daley, Richard J.
(1902–1976) mayor of Chicago, Illinois, from 1955 to 1976

Dylan, Bob
(1941–) musician who performed at the March on Washington

Eisenhower, Dwight D.
(1890–1969) president of the United States from 1953 to 1961

Evers, Medgar
(1925–1963) civil rights activist killed in 1963

Farris, Christine King
(1927–) Martin's older sister

Gandhi, Mahatma
(1869–1948) leader of the Indian independence movement

Johnson, Lyndon B.
(1908–1973) president of the United States from 1963 to 1969

Kennedy, John F.
(1917–1963) president of the United States from 1961 to 1963

Kennedy, Robert F.
(1925–1968) attorney general of the United States; President Kennedy's brother

Kennedy, Ted
(1932–2009) senator who sponsored a bill to make Martin's birthday a holiday

King, Alberta Williams
(1904–1974) Martin's mother

King, Alfred Daniel (A. D.) Williams
(1930–1969) Martin's younger brother

King, Bernice Albertine
(1963–) Martin's younger daughter

King, Coretta Scott
(1927–2006) Martin's wife

King, Dexter Scott
(1961–) Martin's younger son

King, Martin Luther III
(1957–) Martin's older son

King, Martin Luther Sr.
(1899–1984) Martin's father

King, Yolanda Denise
(1955–2007) Martin's older daughter

Luther, Martin
(1483–1546) religious thinker who began the Protestant Reformation

Malcolm X
(1925–1965) leader, speaker, and activist who believed in using violence when necessary

Nixon, Richard M.
(1913–1994) president of the United States from 1969 to 1974

Parks, Rosa
(1913–2005) civil rights activist who played a vital role in the Montgomery bus boycott

Ray, James Earl
(1928–1998) criminal who shot and killed Martin

Reeb, James
(1927–1965) minister who was killed by the Ku Klux Klan in 1965

Thoreau, Henry David
(1817–1862) writer who believed in civil disobedience

Glossary

act
law that the government has passed

activist
someone who takes action against something he or she feels is wrong

assassin
someone who kills a politician or religious leader

bail
money paid to free someone from police custody before he or she stands trial

bill
proposed new law

boycott
form of protest in which someone refuses to deal with a certain person or organization

civil disobedience
using peaceful methods when refusing to follow a law believed to be unfair

civil rights
rights to freedom and equality given by the US Constitution

communist
person who believes that the government should own everything and share its wealth and products between its citizens, or people

confrontation
meeting in which people challenge, or confront, one another

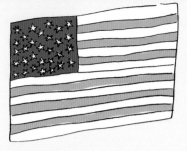

Congress
law-making branch of the US government

constitution
document listing the rights of a nation's citizens and how its government should work

FBI
Federal Bureau of Investigation—part of the US government that investigates crime

federal law
law that applies throughout the United States

ghetto
slum in which people of one religious group or race live

integration
bringing people of different races together to make sure they are treated equally

Jim Crow laws
unfair laws that discriminated against black people

Ku Klux Klan (KKK)
secret society violently opposed to the Civil Rights Movement and its beliefs

martyr
person whose death inspires others to fight for their cause

National Guard
military of a US state

Nobel Peace Prize
medal awarded each year in Oslo, Norway, to a person or group who has worked for world peace

philosopher
someone who thinks deeply about the nature of the world and life

policy
way that something is officially done

protest
to show that you disapprove of, or do not agree with, something

racism
belief that certain people are better than others because of their race, or hating a group of people because of their race

seamstress
woman whose job is sewing

122

segregation
keeping people of different races or religions separate from each other

seminary
school that trains clergy, such as priests

sharecropper
farmer who works a small plot of land owned by another farmer

sit-in
form of protest in which people sit in one place and refuse to leave

slum
poor, crowded, often dirty section of a city

solitary confinement
state of being kept isolated, or on your own, in prison

spiritual
type of religious song

state trooper
member of a US state's police force

strike
when workers refuse to work in order to convince or force their employer to meet their demands

Supreme Court
highest court in the United States

tear gas
chemical that temporarily blinds people by stinging their eyes and producing tears; sometimes used by police to control crowds

Index

Acknowledgments

DK would like to thank: Romi Chakraborty and Pallavi Narain for design support; Lindsay Walter-Greaney for proofreading; Helen Peters for the index; and Jolyon Goddard for additional editorial work.

ANSWERS TO THE QUIZ ON PAGES 116–117

1. 1929; 2. 14 years old; 3. Mohandas Gandhi, or Mahatma Gandhi; 4. Montgomery, Alabama; 5. The National Association for the Advancement of Colored People; 6. *Time* magazine; 7. newspaper and toilet paper; 8. Civil Rights Act; 9. Nobel Peace Prize; 10. Richard J. Daley; 11. "I AM A MAN"; 12. January